SECRETS

Earn $5000 a Month Posting Your Pad

by Sebastian Ritter

A FastReads Publication

TABLE OF CONTENTS

PROLOGUE

Think about this for a second: how would your life change if you can make at least an extra $5,000 in a month?

Perhaps a portion of that amount can go to paying off your mortgage or student loans, take care of your monthly rent, or maybe fund your dream car/business/vacation?

I for one could tell you that life has changed much after I made my first $5,000 renting out my house in Airbnb. Actually, even the average, passive Airbnb host earns $10,000 annually – but who wants to be average? I sure didn't! Instead, I worked towards learning the strategies that will get my listing booked 100% solid every month – and life has never been the same.

But I don't want you to get ahead of yourself here. There are many books written by those who've made bank on Airbnb, but it might not help someone who's about to rent out their *first* property on Airbnb. In this book, I'd like to share with you the secrets I used to earn my first $5,000 on Airbnb, just by renting out a single property.

This reader-friendly guide has 3 easy to follow parts:

• **Part 1**: What you need to prepare before setting up your property, including tricky matters like insurance and taxes

• **Part 2:** How to keep your listing occupied and make as much money as you can

• **Part 3:** How to optimize your business, so you work less hours, but keep your guests pleased

This is your solid guide to starting, growing and scaling your Airbnb business and making your first $5,000 just by renting out your room, home or pad.

INTRODUCTION

The idea of renting out my pad on Airbnb happened through pure happenstance. I was paying mortgage on a two-bedroom apartment, when my transfer to the company's sales department had required me to be on the road more often that when I was home.

Frequent days alone on the road also meant living out of a suitcase and staying in hotels, and as the months passed I increasingly assimilated my new assignment and had enough extra time to explore the cities and neighborhoods I was doing business in. Weekends were spent exploring parks, restaurants, museums, and making new friends away from home.

What was once a lonely assignment had turned into an opportunity for me to explore the country. In my search to make the experience more worthwhile, I discovered the joys of booking an Airbnb instead of a hotel. I loved feeling like a local, and it helped me feel more at home, wherever I was staying.

One night, as I was browsing through Airbnb for my next home in another city, a lightbulb just switched on – I would be renting a 2-bedroom for $130 per night, and all the host had to do was make sure I found the place, and have it in order before my stay! I had the same 2-bedroom apartment at home, only, it was just sitting there waiting for me.

The thought of renting out my place stayed with me. In between moving from city to city, I read all that I could on the internet for tips on how to start an Airbnb business, and immediately got to work once I was back at home. That was 3 years ago, and I haven't looked back since. But it sure would have been easier if I avoided some missteps along the way!

This resource is a summation of everything I had learned since I made my first $5,000 on Airbnb. Through this simple guide, I sincerely hope you achieve the same success I have had.

PART I:
PREPARING FOR YOUR BUSINESS:

How to Set up Your Listing for Success

1. FOOD FOR THOUGHT: Know Why You Want to Start This Business

I believe I would have made my first $5,000 faster if I had a step-by-step resource on setting up the *business* side of Airbnb hosting. I studied a lot of resources available online, but they mainly offer tactics on how to set up your place, how to attract the right market, etcetera.

While those are important, Airbnb is just like any other business – it will benefit from having a plan, a clear direction, and an objective from the start. It also involves taxes and some legalities, which unfortunately most beginners are unprepared for when they start renting their place out. Understanding this part and having a plan in place will save you tons of time, headaches and money in the future. Before you even begin to fix your pad or list it, ask yourself the following questions:

1. What do you want to get out of hosting?

Just by the fact that you picked up this e-book, I can already tell that you want to make extra money. Needless to say, the more money you want to make, the higher the level of dedication you need to put in, at least at the start. Do consider that there are different levels of commitment for an Airbnb business (yes – full time is not the only option!):

• **Opportunity-based:** you only host because you have a spare bed or room, and if there is an impending influx of renters in your area, say, during a music festival, marathon or other events. Obviously, you'll only make a killing during these seasons. This also applies if you don't really have a spare room, but will find a way to make one, just in time for this season.

• **Investor:** this is how those Airbnb millionaires make their money. They are your old-school real estate investors who have extra property or buy property for the purpose of renting out.

• **Rental Business Owners:** this is where most Airbnb hosts fall, and where most of the tips in this book will come from. You either rent out an entire house, or sublet an entire pad in order to make extra money. Our goal is to be fully-occupied every month, in order to meet the $5,000 goal.

2. How much time can you dedicate to hosting?

Having figured out your commitment level using the three items above, you'd need to estimate how much time your business will need. This is especially important if you plan to do Airbnb hosting on the side.

Below are the basic tasks hosts do:

• **Communicating with guests and prospects.** Assume that you will give near real-time responses to inquiries and crafting clear communication and instructions to your place. (*allot 10 minutes per day*)

• **Check-ins and check-outs.** Assume that your logistics may include picking them up from the airport – if you want to go the extra mile. You would also need to ensure that they have a way to get into the house, and that your place is left in the same condition they found it, as property damage and thefts do happen! (*allot 2 hours for every check-out for cleaning and checking items*)

• **Housekeeping.** This would include not just cleaning, but also checking through all items and amenities that must be present for guests. (*allot 15 minutes per day*)

Assume your occupancy for the month and multiply it by the hours above. For example, if you have 1 guest or group per week, then your occupancy is 4. At this rate, you would need:

Communication:	30 days x 10 minutes	=	5 hours
Check-out:	4 checkouts x 2 hours	=	8 hours
Housekeeping:	30 days x 15 minutes	=	7.5 hours

TOTAL: 20.5 hours/month

If you are certain that you can allot this much time to your business, or have someone you can split the tasks with, then you are well on your way to setting up an Airbnb business that generates revenue.

2. LAY THE FOUNDATION: Plan Your Business Well

When I was starting out, many of the resources I read online only covered the physical aspect of running the business – setting up the property, creating a listing, how to do or outsource the housekeeping and maintenance.

These are all important, but Airbnb is just like any other business where there are legal and tax implications. And shouldn't those come before you even set up a business? In this section, we'll go through 4 steps of setting up your Airbnb business:

STEP 1: Defining your Target Market

STEP 2: Keeping yourself protected (Insurance)

STEP 3: Dealing with Neighbors, Landlords, and the Law (Legalities)

STEP 4: Learning about Taxes

STEP 1: Defining Your Target Market

One of the common mistakes I see newbies make on Airbnb is targeting everyone. You may ask, "Isn't that the fastest way to make money on that site? To cater to more people?" From what I've learned, catering to everyone just makes it harder to please *anyone* period. Think about this – a solo backpacker would have different needs from a family, a retired couple, and a group of friends travelling together, right?

I had greater success and less headaches when I identified my ideal guest and aimed straight for them. You can cater to different markets later on, when you widen your range of properties for rent, but I would start with choosing just one or two -- and often that guest is a lot like you. I suggest you begin by learning about the 6 main traveler tribes, through Page 8 of the Amadeus Report found here:

http://www.amadeus.com/documents/future-traveller-tribes-2030/amadeus-traveller-tribes-2030-airline-it.pdf.

Once you've identified the ideal guest/s you want to cater to, attract them by doing the following:

Stage the property to cater to your guests' need.

Let's say you've chosen to host small families and retired couples first, since you figured they're easier to get along with, and are less likely to trash the place. How then do you discourage party animals and young travelers from booking your property? Send a message that it's for families.

Have a well-equipped kitchen and fully-stocked pantry. Provide a few toys and books for kids. Then simply send the message that you welcome families and retired couples only.

Inject your personality into the space.

As said, your first ideal guest will most likely have values and tastes similar to yours, so it's best to decorate the space with your own taste.

Do mind the limitations to this freedom however: avoid adult-oriented or very niched themes as you may attract a very select few. Stick to a neutral theme, then add items from your hobbies. And then, put some local flavor – remember, this is why your guest is booking an Airbnb and not a hotel!

Suggest some local activities that your ideal guest will enjoy.

Think like a tourist and jot down all the things that your ideal guest can do within the vicinity. What are some family-friendly and wholesome activities that are considered must do's in your town? Moreover, highlight what makes your neighborhood ideal to stay in – Very low crime rate? Lots of restaurants or transport options?

When we get to listing your property, we'll tackle how we'll make these details shine.

STEP 2: Keeping Yourself Protected

It's only natural for a first-time host to worry about keeping the property safe, since you're welcoming strangers into it, and most especially if you also live in it.

Airbnb recognizes this concern, and there are various ways to keep yourself protected using their standards and mechanisms. Below are 7 main ways to protect yourself as a host, back-linked to the specific Airbnb page, so you can review them further.

1. Verified IDs

Hosts and guests need to connect or submit an ID to their Airbnb account as proof of identification. This ID can be an online account (like Facebook, LinkedIn or Google+), a government ID, or a home and e-mail address.

Tip: Always look for the verified ID badge before speaking to a prospective guest. You may also ask for added proof of identification before approving their request.

2. Private Messaging

Hosts and guests are required to communicate via Airbnb's chatroom before bookings take place. This allows you to reference and save your communication, just in case.

Tip: You may use texts and emails to communicate with guests after the booking has been confirmed, but it's safer to always use the platform should issues arise.

3. House Rules

Hosts are allowed to create their own house rules. There is a section for this on your Airbnb profile, so guests are informed before they place their reservation.

Tip: Be firm and direct on serious matters parties, drinking, drugs and property damage. I suggest you also politely remind your guest to review these a few days before their stay.

4. Reviews

Hosts and guests can be reviewed via Airbnb. When someone makes an inquiry, you can look at their previous reviews, and see whether the guest will be a good fit for your property or house rules.

Tip: It's fine to decline a guest if you do not feel comfortable with hosting them. One bad review among a majority of good ones would not hurt, however. Look for a pattern of behavior among your guest's previous reviews and weigh whether they will pose a problem.

5. Security Deposits

Hosts can ask guests to make a security deposit (which will be added to their booking fees), to protect you from eventualities like property damage or theft. The value can range from $95 to $5,100, and will be given back to guests if no such incident took place. Note that this has to be added *before* a reservation is made.

Tip: It's best to always add a security deposit, as they are much easier to claim than your own insurance and the Host Guarantee. The best scenario is to never have to use this at all – so always keep valuables out of the home!

6. The $1 Million Host Guarantee

This guarantee is provided by Airbnb to allow eligible hosts to reimburse damages of up to $1,000,000 caused by guests to their possessions or property. There is also a separate Host Protection Insurance.

Tip: Airbnb has strict procedural requirements for submitting a claim, so this may result in failed claims if you don't follow them exactly. Given the stringent requirements involved, it is best to add a security deposit to avoid having to file this claim.

7. 24/7 Customer Hotline

For emergencies, hosts and guests can reach Customer Support directly by dialing *+1-855-424-7262* or *1-855-4-AIRBNB* for the US. For other countries, the local Airbnb number is published in the confirmation e-mail they send you.

Tip: I hope you don't have to use this security measure! If you sense a situation about to arise, you can already raise your concern or suspicion with Airbnb via email. Should there be a real emergency, call local authorities first (like 911).

Use as many of these measures as possible to keep you and your property safe!

STEP 3: Dealing with Neighbors or Landlords

There are now laws concerning Airbnb compared to when the platform first opened, as more states and territories now recognize it as a business. Moreover, there are also legalities involved if you will be renting out a space that you yourself are renting.

Here's how to deal with each of them:

Local Laws

Begin by knowing which local laws affect you before you negotiate with your landlord and before you list your space. Full knowledge of these will make it easier for you to negotiate and get your landlord or neighbor's approval. Check for the following:

• Do you need to obtain a license or permit before you list your property and accept payment?

• Does your type of short-term booking is permitted in your city at all? For example, in New York, only a landowner can sublet their property for less than 30 days - and only if they are residing in the property.

• What are the penalties that apply if you do not abide by laws and regulations? Can you risk paying these penalties if ever?

Tip: Go to the Responsible Hosting page of Airbnb and check for **Your City's Regulations** to see what applies to you.

Landlord Negotiations

There are many like you who have extra space in their rented space, and have to deal with their landlords and neighbors. This complicates the situation a bit, since the decision to rent the space out doesn't depend on you alone. Consider the following when negotiating with your landlord:

What are the risks for your landlord? And how can you convince him that you can mitigate these?

• The most obvious is the risk of property damage, theft, or harassment from guests

• Short-term rentals may be illegal in your municipality, and the landowner may be fined

• In the US, landlords are required to have homeowners' insurance for their property. However, having an Airbnb makes the property a *business* and not a residence – so he becomes ineligible to collect claims.

There are actually more downsides for a landlord, so you'll need to provide something in return.

Do you have good relations with your tenant?

Having a clean record and good history of payment will make it easier to negotiate, obviously.

What can you offer your landlord in exchange?

Ask your landlord which aspect weighs more to him – is it *safety* or *income?* (It's likely both!) You can propose the following:

For *income*:

• Offer to pay rent in advance or make a few months' deposit upfront

• Extend your lease

• Give him a percentage of your Airbnb earnings

For *safety*:

• Explain the Airbnb $1 Million host guarantee

• Offer to get a separate insurance on top of the host guarantee

• Limit rentals to certain days (like weekends), to certain groups (like families only) or to certain conditions (only when you are around)

Neighbor Relations

Your neighbors are likely to buy in if your landlord agreed to your proposal, so talk to them only after everything has been put in writing. Offer information only on the security aspect – let them know if you have guests coming over, and even share the guests' names and schedules with them for their peace of mind.

Tip: Go to the Trust & Safety page on Airbnb's Help Center for more details.

STEP 4: Learn About Taxes

Any profitable venture usually comes tax. While it may be tempting to skip tax, the consequences of getting caught is usually costlier – such as audits, penalties, and a ruined record.

But aside from being a law-abiding citizen, the importance of knowing taxes is necessary for this business. It is particularly important when you compute for your pricing and profit margins.

As a US company, Airbnb is required to collect taxpayer information from customers who earn income in the US. So, when you create your profile, Airbnb will ask for your taxpayer information.

The following information is an attempt to simplify tax processes and requirements. *Always* consult a tax professional for your questions.

Will Airbnb collect and remit my taxes?

It depends where you're located. For now, they collect and remit taxes on behalf of hosts in selected cities only (17 in the US), but are working towards making this available in all cities where Airbnb is present.

Tip: Go to the Full List of Areas with Occupancy and Tax Collection and Remittance. It includes the type of taxes and tax computations for every city. Your location not listed? It means you need to compute and remit your own taxes, for now at least.

What are the taxes that I need to pay?

I had to dig up my Accounting 101 for this one. It taught me that: **Dues – Deductions = Tax Obligations.**

In the case of an Airbnb business:

Federal Tax + Local Tax + Value Added Tax – Deduction / Business Expense = **Tax Obligation**

Not all taxes will apply to everyone, and not everyone will be eligible to make deductions.

• **Federal Income Tax** – Tax applied by the government to your total income.

• **Local Tax** – Tax assessed by your local authority such as a city or state.

• **Value Added Tax** - Tax assessed on the value of goods and services. This *doesn't* apply in the US, but Airbnb charges VAT on its users from the European Union, Switzerland, Norway, Iceland, South Africa and Japan.

• **Tax Deductions** - Expenses that you incurred in setting up the business or to earn income. Declaring these will help you reduce your taxes. Examples are mortgage payments, cleaning fees, etc.

How do I compute for my taxes?

Since Airbnb cannot collect and remit taxes for all hosts yet, they have created an extensive, step-by-step Rental Taxation Guide with international audit firm Ernst & Young.

Tip: Consult the comprehensive Taxes section on Airbnb.

3. SETTING UP YOUR PROPERTY

Now that you're pretty much covered when it comes to pre-business setup work, it's time to get the space ready for occupancy. In Section II, we talked about defining your ideal guest – your space will have to be designed in a way that attracts that guest, in order to keep your space booked 100% of the time.

Have a clean, but immersive space

Most guests book an Airbnb to avoid the cookie-cutter hotels and feel more like a local in your neighborhood. They want to feel as if, even for just a few days or weeks, they really lived in your city. At the same time, you don't want to give them culture shock by being too niched.

To do this, stick to a clean, timeless design (think neutral colors and natural wood), then add statement pieces. Be careful not to put items that are too personal or may alienate the guest, such as personal photos or religious items.

Make them feel at home with complete amenities

Just as guests expect to feel at home in your pad, they expect it to be as equipped for their immediate and basic needs as well. In order for you not to miss anything, I recommend using this checklist of amenities created by Guesty, a concierge and cleaning company that offers services to Airbnb hosts. Do add to this list as you see fit, and tick it off after every round of cleaning in your pad. Also have a fresh sheet ready whenever you do housekeeping.

Impress with a Home and Neighborhood Guidebook

Most newbie hosts don't know this, but Airbnb actually has a built-in Neighborhood Guidebook feature. I consider these one of the best ways to make guests feel that you went above and beyond your duties as host. Apart from having complete amenities, having a guidebook ready on how to navigate your place, and the things to see and do in your neighborhood is an additional bait to get them to book your place.

4. THE ANATOMY OF A GREAT AIRBNB LISTING

Now that the place is ready for occupancy – we'll proceed to the most crucial part of getting your place booked: creating your listing.

This is one of the best-kept secrets of Superhosts and experienced Airbnb landlords. They know that attracting their ideal guest, and keeping their property booked solid is *not an accident.* Rather, it is brought about by creating a listing that piques a prospective guest's interest, making him choose to book that listing above any other.

Here's how to make your listing stand out and rank high on search results:

Use professionally-shot photos.

If you have a digital camera and decent photography skills, well and good. But I suggest you take advantage of Airbnb's free photography service for eligible hosts. They offer this service as data shows that listings that have professionally-taken photos get booked twice as often.

Aside from being free, you'll also get a Verified watermark because a representative of Airbnb has been to your place. Learn about how to sign up for their Free Photography service.

SELF TAKEN	PROFESSIONALLY TAKEN

Photos taken from Airbnb Website

Use a complete but compelling description of your place and neighborhood.

Let all the hard work you put into making the place livable shine in your description! Make it stand out by:

• *Using an enticing and descriptive title.* Describe the ambience, the theme and the neighborhood of your property in one short sentence: *Scandinavian Themed Penthouse in Brooklyn.*

• *Use specific words to describe the amenities.* This will help your prospect picture the place. Avoid vague words like clean, amazing, nice, etc. Use instead *bright and airy, professional grade, open floor plan,* etc.

• *Use headings and bullet points instead of long paragraphs.* You'd want all the pertinent information about your place to be available on your profile, while keeping your prospect's attention. Categorize the information (such as description about The Pad, The Building, The Neighborhood, The House Rules) and break them down into bite-sized pieces.

• *But don't forget to include your House Rules, as well as building rules and regulations.* Guide guests on what is allowed and not allowed in your house and building, using a firm but non-threatening tone.

Create an endearing personal profile.

Aside from the local experience, one of the factors guests look for is the reliability and likability of their hosts. Put yourself in their shoes – aren't you likely to stay with a host whose personality you like and who seems trustworthy?

You would want to talk about the following: what you do / your occupation, why you decided to list your space / whether you live there, your hobbies and interests. Though these may seem personal, these are worth mentioning as it shows that you are not hiding anything. You're likely to make them feel comfortable, even before they meet you!

Tip: Look at some Superhosts in your area or in a nearby city and pick out the ones you like. What common practices do they use in their profiles? You may want to adopt these practices, too.

PART II
MONEY MAKING STRATEGIES:

How to Work Your Way up to $5,000 per month

5. BE SEEN: Catapult Your Listing to the Top of Search Results

Now that you've worked on making a compelling listing, we'll learn about how to ensure that your listing is seen by your ideal guest, and comes up on the first page of every search.

The practices we did in creating your listing already help, but the truth is that every website, Airbnb included, has SEO and algorithm practices in place that you need to know your way around. Here are some things to remember:

Always keep your calendar updated.

Obviously, your bookings will be a mess if you don't update your calendar, and it will turn off customers. One other reason you should keep this updated however, is that Airbnb's algorithm tags hosts who are active, and reward them with priority search rankings.

Use relevant keywords in your property title and description.

This is a classic SEO trick. Use words that tourists are likely to use, specific to your property and location. For example, mention proper names of tourist attractions, local events, major landmarks, and available transportation. Superhosts use this trick all the time.

Have a complete profile.

The SEO ranking of a complete profile is also part of Airbnb's reward system. No to mention, it will encourage prospective guests to go ahead and book you, as it makes you seem more trustworthy.

Respond in a timely manner.

Airbnb's algorithm also rewards response time, and actually penalizes those who don't reply soon enough (within 24 hours). It is possible to sync inquiries to your email and mobile, so this should be an easy task.

Gun for 5 star reviews.

This is a no brainer. The best way to work your way to the top of search results, organically, is to optimize your rankings on Airbnb. This is the backbone of all bookings in Airbnb as it guarantees that you get guests' trust.

6. PRICING IS EVERYTHING: How to Price Your Listing to Earn So Much More

Apart from taxes and legalities, pricing the property correctly is often an overwhelming and confusing part of the Airbnb business. But you shouldn't let the confusion and initial overwhelm deter you from mastering this part – this is actually where you make money.

Airbnb has a built-in pricing calculator, and there are also third-party pricing calculators out there. However, understanding some pricing principles will enable you to understand your business, and crunch numbers to make the most profit possible.

Simple math would tell us that to earn our $5,000 goal, you would have to make $162 per night and have all 31 nights booked.

AVERAGE NIGHTLY PRICE	# OF NIGHTS BOOKED	EARNINGS PER MONTH
$162	31	$5,000

Below, I will teach you how to: (1) determine if your property can be priced at this nightly rate, (2) ensure that your property is booked solid, (3) ways for you to price it higher.

Nightly Price

Once you list your property, you will be asked to give your asking price per night. The price you set is supposed to reflect the size, amenities, and location of your listing.

Airbnb's calculator will suggest a pricing tip based on listings similar to yours, and while you may start with that, I'd suggest making your own pricing down the line. The basis of Airbnb is very limited – what we're after here is your pad's *profitability.*

Airbnb's calculator will look at your location, size (number of bedrooms and baths), property type (apartment, condo, house), and number of guests you can accommodate.

The problem is that there are properties similar to yours in these aspects, but may not be the same quality as your property. You risk over or underpricing then.

Here's how to determine your nightly price:

Step 1: Look at the average nightly price of properties like yours.

Search on Airbnb for properties within your neighborhood, and be as specific as possible. For example, instead of typing *Manhattan, New York,* put *Marble Hill, Manhattan.* Then enter any date, and assume you're having an overnight stay.

Then, the Filter Options will show. Proceed to select all the filters that apply to your listing: *room type, size, amenities* and *property type*.

Your search will show you *the number of listings* in your neighborhood that are just like yours, and *the average price nightly.*

Step 2: Next, look at the average nightly price of properties like yours, for every month of the year.

The season and the number of listings available in your neighborhood should be part of the strategy for determining your pricing. Basically, when there is *more demand* (less properties available), price higher; when there is *more supply* (more properties available), price lower.

Fill up a chart with the following details:

MONTH	# OF LISTINGS	AVERAGE PRICE/NIGHT	YOUR PRICE

I suggest adjusting your price by deducting or adding 5-10% depending on the number of listings and average price per night in your neighborhood.

At the beginning however, I would suggest that you price lower than your competition, just to get the bookings coming in first. Switch to the method above once you have several 5 star reviews.

Tip: Here's a step-by-step guide to Setting Your Base Price.

Special Offer

A Special Offer or simply a discount is a good way to keep your property occupied for longer. Now, you might be asking – wouldn't a discount hurt my earnings? Not if it means that you will have more nights booked.

Let's assume that once you offer a discount, you'll hook a one-week long stay:

WITH DISCOUNT		WITHOUT DISCOUNT	
Nightly Price	$162	**Nightly Price**	$162
Discount	0.10	**Discount**	-
Nightly stays / mo	17 or $2754	**Nightly stays / mo**	17 or $2754
Weekly stays / mo	2 or $2268	**Weekly stays / mo**	1 or $1134
NET INCOME	$5,022 -502.20 **$4,519.8**	**NET INCOME**	**$3,888.00**

Note that Airbnb counts a weekly stay if its lasts for at least 7 nights. The table above shows that even if you discount, if you keep your property booked, you'll still earn more than if you don't discount but don't get a guest.

Increasing

Earlier, we discussed that there can be seasons where your property can be priced higher, such as when there is a large number of tourists – during festivals, conferences, or even during usual peak travel seasons like Christmas. Aside from these instances, weekends are also an opportunity to price higher than your nightly rate, as demand for short-term stays are higher.

Seasonal Pricing

To do this, I suggest making a list of events, conferences, and other occasions that raise the number of tourists in your area. Before you set a higher seasonal price on these dates, do check out the rest of your competition and see if they do this as well. Also, consider whether your *ideal guest* is the market for those events.

I would advise you to implement Seasonal Pricing early on, as travelers tend to book early. At the end of the pricing chapter, we'll also tackle how to set last-minute pricing.

Tip: There is a step-by-step guide to Seasonal Pricing on the AirBnB website.

Weekend Pricing

A good rule of thumb as to whether this will work for you is if the hotels nearby also do Weekend Pricing. As long as you're not priced way higher than most hotels, then it still won't deter guests from booking you.

Airbnb's pricing calculator suggests making a 15-30% increase when it comes to Seasonal or Weekend pricing, but I would again suggest doing 5-10% first if you're new.

Last Minute Pricing

The last pricing strategy you can implement is to adjust it based on your remaining available dates for the month. Remember, more supply – price lower, more demand – you can price higher.

The same principle applies when it comes to your calendar:

Farther from date – higher price

Nearer the date – lower price

What you want to do is lower your prices just enough so that your remaining unbooked dates would be filled.

Tip: AirBnb offers a guide to Smart Pricing on their website.

The four strategies above are the basics of pricing your property right, in order for you to make your income goal every month. As you get to know your market, it wouldn't harm to make your own pricing strategies, or hike up your increases, as you see fit.

7. GETTING PAID

Of course, a crucial part of this business is understanding how to get your earnings from Airbnb, safely and easily.

How does Airbnb pay me?

All bookings need to be processed and paid via the Airbnb platform. It may be tempting to conduct this outside Airbnb (and avoid service charges), but doing so may put you in danger. Moreover, it's a breach of their Terms of Service, which could mean you will be banned from the platform.

Basically, there are 5 steps to getting paid on Airbnb:

1. You choose a Payout Method

2. Guest pays on Airbnb

3. Airbnb calculates the Payout (with taxes and service fee deducted)

4. Airbnb releases the money after check-in

5. Host withdraws Payout

What is the best Payout Method?

There are currently 5 options available for getting your payments processed. Choose the most convenient one for you.

ACH or Direct Deposit – direct deposit to your Savings or Checking account. To sign up for this, you need to provide both your account number and routing number, which you can get from your bank. Average processing time is 3 business days.

International Wire Transfer – deposit of money to your account through a money transfer system. To sign up, you may need to provide your account number or IBAN, which you can get from your bank. Banks may charge a certain fee. Average processing time is 3-7 business days.

Payoneer Bank Transfer / Debit Card – Create a Payoneer account or have Airbnb transfer to your existing account. Payoneer will have to approve your details before you can receive payouts – always use the same name that you use on your ID to avoid problems. Banks may charge a certain fee. Average processing time is 1 business day.

Paypal – Create a Paypal account or have Airbnb transfer to your existing account. You will be asked for your PayPal account which happens to be an email address. Paypal charges 2.9% + $0.30 for every transaction, and withdrawal fees for non-US banks. Average processing time is 1 business day.

Western Union – collecting your payment via the nearest Western Union branch. To register, you'll need to enter your full name (first, middle, last) in the Western Union system. Always use the same name that you use on your ID to avoid problems. Fees will apply. Average processing time is 1 business day.

Lastly, there you can set a minimum amount that needs to be available in your Airbnb account for you to be able to withdraw. This is optional, and if you set a minimum, Airbnb will hold your payments until you accumulate that amount. This is ideal if your bank charges for every transaction – you'll be saving on fees by withdrawing less frequently, but in larger amounts.

Computing your Payout

In addition to setting your Nightly Price, knowing what Airbnb will deduct (in terms of taxes and service charges), will enable you to compute how much you'll be making per booking, and for the entire month. To do this, follow the table below:

ADD TOGETHER:	SUBTRACT:
Number of nights or weeks booked x Nightly Price + Extra Guest Fee (if applicable)	Airbnb Service Fees
Cleaning Fee (if applicable)	Currency Exchange
	Local Taxes
	Government Taxes

= YOUR PAYOUT

PART III
OPTIMIZE YOUR BUSINESS:

How to Scale the Business to Save More Time and Money

At this point, we've already tackled how to plan your business, setup your property, and make money through different pricing strategies. The key to a thriving Airbnb business that consistently makes $5,000 monthly however, is maintenance—that is, not resting on your laurels and making sure that the experience is delightful for every guest.

In this section, we'll tackle several ways for you to run your Airbnb business more smoothly, and with less stress.

8. SELECTING THE RIGHT GUESTS

Choosing the Right Guests

We've already profiled your ideal guest, so here are a few more reminders in order to determine whether it would be good to accept that reservation:

Choose the guests with a complete profile.

As with hosts, the more information the guest provides, the better you'll be able to gauge whether they fit your criteria for an ideal guest.

Look for their Verified ID badge.

Like hosts, guests are also asked by Airbnb to provide identification. A Verified ID badge is a good indication, but you can still ask for more proof of identification (like a government ID or social media account.

See if you have common friends.

Did you know? Airbnb has a built-in feature that lets you check whether you have mutual friends with a guest on Facebook, Google+ and LinkedIn.

Check out their previous reviews.

Their reviews may help you establish a pattern of peculiarities or behavior that a guest has. Quirks (such as a crying baby, or a penchant for evening karaoke) aren't bad – you just have to gauge whether you, or your neighbors, would be fine with them.

Ask for references.

All Airbnb users can add references to their profile. If your guest has none, it's perfectly acceptable to ask, and you can always say its part of your standard operating procedures.

Declining a Bad Fit

Likewise, there may be telltale signs that a guest may cause you headaches. Look for the following red flags:

He wants to communicate or transact outside of Airbnb. Airbnb provides systems and regulations to protect all users—you risk losing these once you engage with a guest outside the platform.

He does not respond to your questions or refuses to provide additional references or verification. An ideal guest would understand why you are asking for these, and would be willing to give them, if they have nothing to hide.

He has a lot of questions about surveillance in your building or neighborhood. Always trust your instincts. If something feels dodgy, it is best to avoid it.

9. MAINTAINING THE PLACE

As we tackled in Part 1, you'd have to exert a considerable amount of time in maintaining your place. This can be more easily managed over time, once you've set a documented housekeeping system, and even consider outsourcing some of the work.

Here are some ways to ease the work involved in maintaining the place, while still making it conducive for delighting guests:

Incorporate some housekeeping in your House Rules

It is perfectly fine to ask the guests to do some of the upkeep on their own. You may choose to enlist the help of someone, such as a daily cleaner, to do everything for them (for a fee of course!), but you can give guests some reminders in order to make housekeeping flow smoothly. Some examples are:

• Rinsing the dishes and putting them in the dishwasher

• Putting used towels or linens in the laundry bin so you know when to replace them

• Asking them to wipe sinks, mirrors and shower doors dry after using

• Turning off the lights and air-conditioning when they leave

All these, plus other rules that apply, should be on your profile (under House Rules) and in your Home and Neighborhood Guidebook. So as not to put off guests, always use a friendly manner of explaining, and try to provide some rationale as to why they are being asked to do these things.

Document and setup a Housekeeping System or Process

This is one aspect of the business that is hard at first, but gets better with practice. I did go through a period where I'd spend lots of time and energy in making sure the place is perfect for the next guest, but I managed to put a process in place where everything runs like a well-oiled machine. Here are some tips to do that:

• **Make your own Housekeeping checklist.** Aside from the Amenities Checklist I shared before, this is ideal to have whenever you or someone you hired cleans the place.

You may start with Airbnb's Cleaning Checklist, then make a more detailed one that takes you or the cleaner through a step-by-step process of what should be cleaned and what they should look like before check-in.

This makes sure you don't miss a spot!

• **Get someone's help in estimating the time needed to complete housekeeping.** Practice the cleaning, check-in and check-out process and see where you can be more efficient.

Outsourcing your property maintenance

Down the line, I was able to stumble upon some companies who specialize in servicing Airbnb businesses—and this is one of the best business investments I've made. Once you're comfortable with your first property, outsourcing your maintenance and day-to-day work can help you scale to your next Airbnb properties.

There are two types of companies so far that offer these services: First are Concierge Services, who handle cleaning and check-in / check-out processes. Second are Property Management Services, who handle your entire operations, beginning from managing your booking and communicating your guests.

Examples of these companies are Cityami, Handy and Proprly. Be sure to check first if they operate in your area, and assess which services you'd be comfortable to outsource at the moment.

10. GETTING STERLING REVIEWS, AND HANDLING BAD ONES

All your hard work in planning, setting up and getting your Airbnb business off the ground will be wasted if you cannot sustain it. The lifeblood of keeping an Airbnb business alive is in delighting guests, and there is no better measure of this than your reviews.

Here's how to ensure that your guests provide good feedback about you and your property every time:

How hosts are reviewed

Airbnb uses 6 criteria in reviewing hosts: *accuracy, communication, cleanliness, location, check-in* and *value.* After every stay, they send an invitation for each guest to review you and your place based on these aspects.

To ensure a good outcome, keep the following in mind:

Accuracy of Listing

This means how close to reality your listing is. While your listing description and photos should be inviting, it also should not be too far from the guest's actual experience. To ensure this:

• Call out some possible quirks in your profile, such as those that you think may pose a potential issue with guests. Examples are ongoing constructions nearby, a neighbor's noisy dog, you get the idea.

• Be as thorough as possible in your listing. Give your guests the best picture possible of what it's like staying in your place, while being truthful.

Cleanliness and Hygiene

This is where a Housekeeping system comes in handy. Avoid booking back-to-back stays, and give yourself enough time to make sure the place has been cleaned thoroughly before the next guest comes.

Communication

This refers to how responsive you are to your guests, and how accessible you were during their stay. I suggest giving them an alternative way to contact you aside from Airbnb, and checking on them from time-to-time during their stay.

Location

This refers to the overall appeal of your neighborhood, in terms of safety, accessibility, and desirability. This is actually beyond your control, but there are ways to help your guest navigate your neighborhood more easily. One way is creating a Neighborhood Guidebook, as discussed in Part 2.

Value

This refers to whether guests think your property was value for money. Your Amenities Checklist, Neighborhood Guidebook and Housekeeping System helps take care of this—but you can always go the extra mile. Some hosts give welcome gifts, and even go as far as fetching guests from the airport. Think of an extra service that will feel comfortable for you.

Check-in Process

This refers to the ease of check-in and check-out. Now, your place may be great to stay in, but it will hurt your review if it is very hard to get to. To avoid this, help guests get to your place—find out how they will arrive and provide detailed instructions in finding your place.

Moreover, if you cannot handle the check-in and check-out process yourself, make sure that someone capable will be present.

As you begin to receive reviews, take each comment as feedback, and a chance for you to improve your Airbnb business.

How to handle bad reviews

If you get a bad review—relax. Even Superhosts have their moments. At some point, you are bound to get one bad apple, or even slip up sometimes. In any case, you can always bounce back!

Always look at the bright side: don't you think that hosts with zero bad reviews arouse suspicion? The good thing about reviews is that it allows you to respond and explain yourself.

When you do get that (hopefully just one) bad review, do the following:

• **DON'T** reply immediately! Calm yourself down first.

• **DO** take time in crafting a response. Use a tone that is polite, non-confrontational, and one that acknowledges your guests feelings and concerns.

• **DO** address all the concerns that your guest raised. Subsequent guests will likely read this, and will be interested in how you will fix the issue. If you believe that there was a misunderstanding, then by all means provide your perspective.

• **DO** offer a subsequent stay that addresses the issue, or with a discount. This further shows that you are committed to providing good service.

One bad review does not mean the end of your Airbnb business. Handle it with composure, and focus on providing the best service you can. A good guest knows a good host when they see it.

Thank you and good luck!

My intention for creating this resource is to help give you the head start you need in setting up your Airbnb business. It's a discovery that has truly changed my life, and not just in terms of money—Airbnb is a lucrative business, but it's also a diverse community you would love to be part of. Meeting people from around the world, providing good service, and making money in the process is an opportunity that has never been available until recently. I wish you success as you embark on the journey of being an Airbnb entrepreneur!

END

If you enjoyed this summary, please leave 5 stars and an honest review on Amazon.com!

Here are some other available titles from FastReads we think you'll enjoy:

Summary of Impossible to Ignore: by Carmen Simon, PhD

Summary of The Hard Thing About Hard Things: by Ben Horowitz

Budget Travel Secrets: A Step-by-Step Guide for Traveling Better, Longer, for Less

Travel Hacking Secrets: The Definitive Beginner's Guide to Travel Hacking and Flight Hacking